Love and Loss

Christopher White

Typesetting by Rack and Rune Publishing
rackandrune.com

Contents

Oceans of Tears

No-one sees you crying in an ocean.
The tang of tears or water, who can tell?
The sound of sobbing smothered by the swell
As waves of sadness wash across your face.

Grief, the undertow of the emotion,
Unbearable the weight can drag you down.
It's tugging at your feet until you drown
To sink and disappear without a trace.

The brininess contradicts that notion.
Increasing with the tears that have been shed,
And gaining greater buoyancy instead,
The more the salt for water we replace.

Float at first. Then rocking in slow motion.
By gently moving hands from side to side.
Kick with arms outstretched until you glide
Toward the shore to find a safer place.

The Rose

Though I may seem remote, do not condemn
My heart unkind incapable of love
When in defence like thorns upon a stem
I guard this rose. As roses stand above
Their barbs and bloom so too do I defend
My heart from thieves who steal and then discard.
Who in their wanton pleasure petals rend
And leave denuded love forever scarred.
If you can hold a rose and disregard
The callous cuts unthinking thorns inflict
And hide your hurt behind a brave façade
Denying you have by a spike been pricked
Then take this rose and disregard the pain
Of distant thorns. You will not love in vain.

The Vow

The day, the dress, the cake, the kiss
celebrating wedded bliss
and the moment that exists
to mark the union that it is.

But of one thing we can be sure.
moments merge into years. And for
the unsuspecting human heart
we grow together or apart
when time and circumstances pull
at our intentions. Purposeful
are the couples who can say
I love you more than I did this day.

They say "I love you" and
"You love me" too.
Over and over and over because
the vow is a wish that repeated comes true.

If I could

If I could climb the highest peak
Higher than a bird can fly
As thrilling as that is, still I
Couldn't stay where I cannot breathe.

If I could plumb the deepest depths
Where Davey Jones' locker lies
The sunken treasures left behind
Air and time compressed to leave.

If I could sing the sweetest song
And everybody sang along
I fear that it would not be long
Before I performed something new.

If I could write the purest line
Flawless rhythm, perfect rhyme
A guard against the march of time
the only thing that it would do.

But I have felt and know true love,
Now and for eternity.
It's where I want and need to be
And I have shared that love with you.

Bridget's Song

"Love is patient and kind
Delights in the truth,
Ready to excuse, trust and hope
And to endure whatever comes."

Words are bountiful or blind
to true meaning or untruth.
A kaleidoscope
of sound where the outcomes

may not be what we expect.
Awkward and inept,
seeking to explore
how best to express

my love for you. I suspect,
in my heart where it is kept,
I could only use words more
if my love for you was less.

Happiness

We've been given one command
to try and love our fellow man
and though I do not understand
the how or why or eternal plan
I do know this
that happiness
is loving you.

In Our Parents Name

Our parents' names
Are shared among
Brothers, sisters,
Daughters, sons.

What our parents once taught us
We are now passing on.
Like a wheel that slowly spins
Another cycle has begun.

What we mean is what we say.
What we say will be done.
In the kingdom of the mind
The generations merge as one.

An identity the crown
Sought and found, lost or won,
From the lessons we have learned
And the races we have run.

As a new day somewhere dawns
From the setting of the sun
What our parents mean to us
Are the people we become.

The Last Act

The flame of life will flicker
when our precious grip, so frail,
weakens in its grasp
and our bodies start to fail
beyond the realm of science
or a surgeon's futile knife.
Life is lived in seasons
and the winter of our life
will see us wither, waste and wilt
like lilies in a pond.
We flower on this earth
to be just as quickly gone.

Age appears to many to be
a plight we can't defeat
but its victory is hollow,
for my memories are sweet
and always will live on
of a race superbly run.
In the outcome of the contest
I see it's you who won.
For you bore your loss of function
with never much ado
and concern and love for others
repeatedly shone through.

If any felt unsettled
by your frailty fault was theirs
as you fought approaching failure
with a grit that none compares.
To be born is to die.
It's a fact from which we run
but you faced it as it was
and didn't come undone.
With that brave acceptance
at last, serenity
was borne upon your face
for one and all to see.

Therefore, dear Patricia
we can so surely say
this world was all the better
for you having passed our way.
We feel it is a privilege
to say that we have known
a lady of great virtue;
in your passing we have grown.
You have taught us all a lesson
with serene simplicity
that the only way to live
is with grace and dignity.

If the meaning is unclear
but our purpose, to be useful,
Life's magic is the love and awe
we have for other people.
And what should be conveyed
in this simple sad oration
is to know and recognise
you deserve a grand ovation.
Even though we mourn the loss
of a mother, friend and wife
we salute the courage shown
in your last great act of life.

Valentine's Day

I dreamt that I was Don Juan
And swept you off your feet
And covered you with kisses
As Casanova would
Until I woke and found that I
Was as I was before.
Alone, yet cold convention
Unable to discard.

For dreams like these are unfulfilled
While heart and head compete
To tie my tongue. Alas I do not
Say the things I should
Nor do what should be done. Though
I would like to say much more
Than these lines allow, and do much
More than send this simple card.

My Favourite Thing

You're my favourite person.
That nothing else can beat.
A perfect picture puzzle
With none of the pieces gone.

My favourite set of colours.
A palate that's complete.
An oscar winning movie
Every time it's shown.

My favourite thing to do
and chosen occupation
is the be and stay with you.
So, wherever we may roam

My favourite place to be
and final destination
is to go to where you go too.
It's the place that I call home.

Stars and Scars

Every cut leaves a scar.
Every battle a bruise.
If no-one truly wins a war,
the more we fight, we lose.

Revenge is bittersweet
when settling a score
if no-one is left unscathed
or better than before.

Set aside the sorrow
with time enough to grieve.
The ones who love us still will be
the ones who still believe

our purpose and our plan.
To be the shining light
cast the smallest shadow.
Your star is shining bright.

Five Sonnets

From origins the same or set apart
We like two lines will have no common bond
If we diverge and differ from the start
Each to the other is a vagabond.
So too two lines askew may intersect
And married for a while one point agree
But transient serve only to dissect
When they as one no longer wish to be.
More similar are two lines parallel.
But though both in the same direction run
They never meet. All chance of love dispel
When hearts untouching never beat as one.
A special love I seek, a single line
Coincident and congruent with mine.

Behold this seed and see in it asleep
the latent force of life. A dormant vault
that we may open and a harvest reap
or leave unsown to die and life default.
If you can see the oak inside the 'corn
that will with rain and light become a tree
and that to grow all must from seeds be born
then woman sow your seeds of love in me.
For you will find I am a fertile field
where rivers of devotion gently flow
and tenderness and passion plough to yield
whatever flowers from your love may grow.
For love can live or die and like a seed
will only bloom when from it shell it's freed.

Loves' colours are kaleidoscopic. They
with mood and minutes, chance and miles, change
from red to blue and back. They often may
across the spectrum of our reasons range.
For love is not a static thing. But then
the wind will still from different angles blow
and rivers may appear to alter when
they change their course yet still as rivers flow.
No, though it may along its spectrum shift
Love doesn't die; if lost, we love again.
But there is, more than love a greater gift
that we can give; and can't, betrayed, regain.
As sails may flap or fill upon a mast
When one is honest love can change and last.

For fate will like haphazard zephyrs tease
with love. Which like a sail when it is blown
can either brightly billow in the breeze
or break and tear. Love needs a solid mast
of loyalty and wants secure cleats
that tempest torn can hold the sail fast
when honest heart and trust entwine as sheets.
No broken mast has ever held aloft
Love's noble shrouds. And when life's gales prove
once loyal timbers under stress are soft
our ships without their sails cease to move.
While we as windswept ships, on sails rely,
Love cannot, unsupported, storms defy.

When you and I united dare defy
whatever fickle fortunes care to cast
against us and events attempt to pry
our love apart I hope our love will last
and like a lighthouse, storm assailed, shine.
While tempest wind and wave and rain may mock
us, resolutely with your hand in mine,
we'll stand secure in our love, a rock.
Yet not of rock. For when a stone is split
in two each fragment will remain a stone
and go their separate way. But how could we
from what was whole be broken and each bit
still be the same? To live unloved alone
and incomplete. Love, halved, will cease to be.

Fishbowl

When did you last say, "I love you"?
It's the best way to show that you care
For your children, your parents and partners
And yourself if you want to be fair.

Tell them how much you need them.
How your lonely heart would follow
wherever their life may lead them.
Yesterday, today and tomorrow.

Tell them how much you miss them.
Every time they walk out the door,
It's the joy they get when you kiss them
Returning to you once more.

Like a fish in a bowl that forgets
every time that it circles around.
When did you last say "I love you"
As silly as that may sound.

I can't tell you enough, if you love them
It's a mantra to keep on your mind.
It's the gift that given away
Will come back to you, you'll find.

Joy

It's a joy to me unmeasured
when I think of you. I found
all I want and will ever need
warmly wrapped around
me and I could not bear to be
without. One with whom
I have ceased to play charades
as all the faces I assume
to hide true feeling, fall away.
To whom to love is not a game
and whose needs and expectations
and desires are the same.

Another who will live with me
and knows and understands
my many moods and feelings.
Who makes little her demands
and most her gifts. A gentle teacher
and a guide who helped me learn
how to cherish love. And loved
how then to love her in return.

Whose love is fierce and loyal
and cannot be won or bought.
Trusted keeper of my secrets
who can read my every thought
without a word between us.
Who in times of need is there
as my confidant, close companion
and my best friend. Who can share
with me my fortunes and misfortunes,
awkward times of doubt and strife
and keep smiling. Who can laugh at
little ironies in life

and shrug them off as unimportant.
Who will share the ups and down
and stand beside me and support me still,
when all and sundry frown
at my mistakes. Who won't desert me
when the going gets too tough
and doesn't want for more but
has and sees in me, enough.

One who simply with her presence
makes my heart inside me swell.
Who can comfort and console me
and make me laugh as well,
making memories that more precious.
Who can look at me and tell
me what I'm thinking. Cherished
more than I care for myself
and for whom I'd do as much as
she would do for me, and more,
without a reservation or
a need to keep a score.

One with whom the love between us
burns, an ever-lasting flame,
forging bonds that can't be broken
and that time and fate can't tame.
One whose needs and expectations
and desires are the same
and no longer one apart is
one in spirit and in name.

Without you who am I?

The tortoise and the turtle
both upon a shell rely
to save them when in danger.
And grains of wheat and rye
when covered by a kernel
as seeds in safety lie.
Yet should we ever take the two
and guard from guarded pry
then each without the other
would un-needed wilt and die.

As answers need a question,
a plane its wings to fly
and mothers need their children,
the sun and stars the sky
we all depend on others.
We need help to get us by
our trials and tribulations.
The demons we defy.

Yet like a land devoid of rain,
a desert barren-dry,
some men hard hearted cannot feel
and tearless cannot cry.
Alone and unfulfilled they're
incomplete and that is why
I cannot be without you.
For without you who am I?

Love and loss.

Remember when we fell in love.
The flush of that first kiss.
Discover then as passions fade
And I wistfully reminisce
Among the desires that we still have
is the one that I'd most miss.

Never Saying Never or No

When what I thought I knew, isn't so
I never say never and never say no.

And the more I learn the less I know,
I never say never and never say no.

When the more I try the worse I go,
with all the effort and nothing to show,
I never say never and never say no.

Or playing to keep and reap what I sow
but cannot gather what didn't grow,
I never say never and never say no.

The hare was fast and the tortoise slow.
Never said never and never said no.

A damaged fighter with a knockout blow.
Never said never and never said no.

Thin ice above the lake below,
An avalanche with one flake of snow.
Never say never and never say no.

When love is lost, our hearts harden. Though
the kindest acts give the warmest glow.
So, never say never and never say no.

The lines of my face.

Though I know the right words
I cannot write them down
like I did. Love's a song I can't sing
as I once sung before.
When I cringe at the sound
of the words and the memories they bring.
No, I can't put the words
in my heart on a page.
I'll not trade away poems for pain
as I foolishly did at
a brave younger age
and leave myself open again.

Love I hide. But I find
that I cannot conceal
it all. Eyes in their silence convey
all the care and respect
and the love that I feel,
all the words I'm reluctant to say.
So, if you conclude
when I don't as I ought
say the things that I should you've no place
in my life, look for words
that unsaid still are thought
and you'll read in the lines of my face.

Good Enough

Everyone has a cross to bear,
A pebble in their shoe.
There are things I wish I hadn't done
And always more to do.

It's the fog that doesn't lift.
The stain I can't remove.
Nothing is ever good enough.
I have something more to prove.

Be careful what you wish for.
Be wise the path you choose.
Diminishing returns can mean
The more you try you lose.

Things that have a sticker price
can have a hidden cost.
An opportunity taken
is a second option lost.

Hold tight the ones who love you
and disregard the rest.
Your best is good enough
when they know it was your best.

A letter to my son

Lie on your back in a field of grass
or on the sand with the surf pounding
And look up into the night sky.
As you peer back in time
stars that no longer exist
Sparkle.

As light travels earthward gaze and ponder this.
All life on Earth will end.
Our Sun's supernova will expand engulfing Earth.
Life must perish on this planet.
So here is the biggest of questions.
If all life, your life, so precious
And a miracle to me
Is destined to end was it pre-destined to start?

Pre-destiny proves planning.
A divinity.
Intelligent men and women argue
objective evidence to the contrary.
But absence of evidence is not proof
that evidence does not exist.
Until the light from an exploding star
reveals the truth we believe it exists
When it does not.

The converse could be equally true.
How you choose to answer that question
influences everything in your life
From that point.
There is only yes or no.
No thought, no idea, don't care,
don't know, is no by default.

Yes, is proactive. Yes, chooses faith.
I choose to believe that your life
is not an accident. I believe your life
Has meaning.
You may not know what that meaning is,
Only that it exists.
Should you be fortunate and find it,
the insight will strike
with sparkling clarity.

A clue. Perhaps life IS the original sin!
Beyond a certain phylogenetic level
Life is cannibalistic.
It consumes itself to promote itself
in a futile self-perpetuating ritual that
Must ultimately fail.

If life is selfish, what is love?
Love makes no sense. Love does not
Favour itself.
It helps the handicapped,
assists the disadvantaged and seeks to
Stop exploitation.

Yet love exists. Imagine your life without it.
For some, perhaps many,
Life is loveless.
Of all the gifts that I've been given,
goals achieved and lessons learned
The single most important thing I have
is my marriage.
Where I have been loved, learnt to love
and about love, where it comes from
And what it means.

"He who loves this life will lose it"
It is plausible to me, dumbstruck as I was
at my microscopic moment of creation
That no proof "exists"
And nothing has been "said" because
nothing could be said that would satisfactorily
Explain anything
Or everything or rob us of the
joy and excitement when we
Discover it ourselves.

Chris the challenges your generation face
Are enormous.
Unsustainable pressures mount
and life will cannibalise itself to survive
As it always has
And will continue to do so
until life is itself unsustainable.

This world, your world, will need
good strong-minded men and women
With courage, conviction, leadership,
 wisdom and compassion.
Let love guide you gently
on that journey. Because
God IS love.

www.ingramcontent.com/pod-product-compliance
Lightning Source LLC
Chambersburg PA
CBHW031547060726
47590CB00004BA/1538